D0227101

Succeeding at Assessment Centres

in a week

JOHN SPONTON
STEWART WRIGHT

Hodder & Stoughton

A MEMBER OF THE HODDER HEADLINE GROUP

499615256

Acknowledgements

Reproduction of test materials

The publishers and authors would like to thank the following for their kind permission to reproduce materials:

SHL (UK) Limted, The Pavilion, 1 Atwell Place, Thames Ditton, Surrey KT7 0NE. Tel: 0870 070 8000. Website: www.shlgroup.com

ASE, Chiswick Centre, 414 Chiswick High Road, London W4 5TF. Tel: 020 8996 3337. Website: www.ase-solutions.co.uk

Orders: please contact Bookpoint Ltd, 130 Milton Park, Abingdon, Oxon OX14 4SB.
Telephone: (44) 01235 827720, Fax: (44) 01235 400454. Lines are open from 9.00–6.00, Monday to Saturday, with a 24 hour message answering service. Email address: orders@bookpoint.co.uk

British Library Cataloguing in Publication Data
A catalogue record for this title is available from The British Library

ISBN 0 340 857676

First published   2002
Impression number   10 9 8 7 6 5 4 3 2 1
Year   2007 2006 2005 2004 2003 2002

Typeset by SX Composing DTP, Rayleigh, Essex.
Printed in Great Britain for Hodder & Stoughton Educational, a division of Hodder Headline Plc, 338 Euston Road, London NW1 3BH. by Cox & Wyman Ltd, Reading, Berkshire.

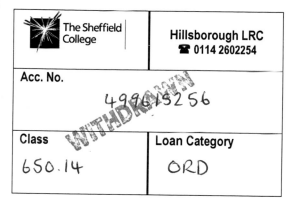

The leading organisation for professional management

As the champion of management, the Chartered Management Institute shapes and supports the managers of tomorrow. By sharing intelligent insights and setting standards in management development, the Institute helps to deliver results in a dynamic world.

Setting and raising standards

The Institute is a nationally accredited organisation, responsible for setting standards in management and recognising excellence through the award of professional qualifications.

Encouraging development, improving performance

The Institute has a vast range of development programmes, qualifications, information resources and career guidance to help managers and their organisations meet new challenges in a fast-changing environment.

Shaping opinion

With in-depth research and regular policy surveys of its 91,000 individual members and 520 corporate members, the Chartered Management Institute has a deep understanding of the key issues. Its view is informed, intelligent and respected.

For more information call 01536 204222 or visit www.managers.org.uk

CONTENTS

■ I N T R O D U C T I O N ■

It is Sunday morning, and you have had a sleepless night. You have covered the whole range of emotions in your restless mind. Somehow, you just do not fancy your usual bowl of cornflakes today. Yesterday a key letter came in the post, the job of your dreams is within reach – or you thought it was!

The letter said that, following your recent job interview, you have been invited to an 'Assessment Centre'. You were initially delighted that you had been successful at the interview, but now you are starting to think more about the next hurdle – the Assessment Centre.

You have heard a mixture of stories about Assessment Centres, sometimes also called Assessment Events, Selection Days, or Extended Interviews. It is true that employers are increasingly using them, but for some candidates the thought of attending causes anxiety and may lead them to drop out of the process and miss a great career opportunity. This is a great pity, because the employer inviting you to an Assessment Centre clearly feels you may have the skills that they are looking for. They just want to find out more about you, and to let you find out more about them.

Perhaps attending an Assessment Centre will be a new experience for you. Alternatively, you may have been to one before, but you realise that your performance could be improved with the benefit of some hints and tips on preparing for the day. Either way, this book is for you and will help you to succeed at an Assessment Centre.

You have already taken the first step by opening this book. Well done! Preparation in advance and an anticipation of situations that might occur are key skills that employers value – particularly in Assessment Centres. Alongside that preparation, a greater familiarity with the workings of an Assessment Centre will also ensure that you are ahead of the game on the day.

In this book we will look in more detail at the type of exercises that you are likely to encounter. There will be plenty of practical hints and tips to help you give your best on that all-important Assessment Centre day.

The scope of this book covers:

- The Assessment Centre process
- Preparing for interviews
- Preparing for group exercises
- Preparing for psychometric tests and questionnaires
- Preparing for presentation exercises
- Preparing for analysis exercises
- Pulling it all together

The Assessment Centre process

What is an Assessment Centre?

An Assessment Centre is not a new phenomenon, but they have been used more and more frequently since the late 1980s onwards. They are often the final hurdle in the selection process and tend to occur after an initial interview or series of interviews, and after an assessment of your application documents. The Assessment Centre is used to build up a picture of your key strengths against a 'template' of what is required to do the job well.

Assessment Centres consist of a series of different selection exercises. They also involve a number of different assessors or interviewers. These assessors are often managers, human resources (HR) or personnel staff and possibly even external consultants, hired by the employer to help out on the day.

Assessment Centres vary in length. They range from around half a day up to two days' duration, depending on the role and its seniority. On average, most events tend to be around one day in duration. You may find that the Assessment Centre is held at the employer's premises, or alternatively off-site at a hotel or another similar venue.

So far so good. One thing you will quickly notice is that other candidates who also applied for the role(s) will be attending the Assessment Centre at the same time as you. You may feel this is awkward or off-putting. Don't worry; we will give some useful hints and tips on this. In the meantime, the key thing to focus upon is that the other candidates will feel the same. Show them the common courtesies and be yourself. Also, remember that other candidates are usually always

present in any recruitment process – you just do not always meet them!

Why have Assessment Centres become more popular?

The key reasons behind the increasing popularity of Assessment Centres are their accuracy, objectivity and fairness.

What are employers looking for?

By the time you attend an Assessment Centre, the employer will have thought carefully beforehand about the job in question, the tasks involved and the objectives of the role. This will help them to think about the type of person they need to perform the job well. They will have created a picture of the ideal person to perform the job, defined by the person's experience, knowledge, skills, personality style and other attributes.

This collection of qualities – experience, knowledge, skills, personality style and other characteristics – are often developed into 'Competencies'. Each Competency is written down as precisely as possible, and in such a way that an assessor knows exactly what to look for when assessing a particular candidate.

For example, part of a definition for a Competency called 'Communication' might include the phrase, 'speaks clearly and concisely'. In an Assessment Centre, the assessors will be looking for evidence of a candidate's ability to speak clearly and concisely, as well as any other aspect of the definition, during the various exercises.

A fuller example of how some employers may define a related Competency called 'Oral communication' is shown below:

Competency – Oral communication
Positive indicators:

- Speaks clearly and concisely
- Speaks confidently on both a one-to-one and group level
- Utilises facts and information to influence others
- Promotes own ideas
- Convinces others and wins them round to own point of view

It is, however, important to note that the exact definitions of Competencies do differ across employers and from level to level. Competencies for the same level of role can be defined very differently across employers, often reflecting the diversity of their businesses. Nevertheless, an example of a broad Competency 'menu' – applicable for a range of professional and managerial roles – can be found in Appendix 1.

You will now appreciate how important it is to have as much information as you can about the job, and in particular the Competencies required to perform the job well. A key aspect of preparing for an Assessment Centre is to gather as much of this information as you can. On Saturday we will spell out the key information you need to obtain to help you in this process.

What typical exercises can I expect?

Employers have a very wide range of exercises upon which they can draw in order to get information about the different

Competency areas. They will choose the methods that they feel are most relevant to the job and that are most likely to give you the opportunity to display the Competencies.

In the list below, you can see the most commonly used exercises. However, do not panic! It is *extremely unlikely* that you would be asked to undertake all of these in one Assessment Centre. Instead, you will probably be asked to undertake a minimum of two exercises, and probably no more than half a dozen.

Each and every one of the exercises will be discussed in more detail during the course of the week.

- Interviews: based around your track record, your experience and/or key Competency areas.
- Group exercises: a team activity based around a practical task or discussion exercise.
- Psychometric tests: standardised tests proven to measure as accurately as possible specific skills and abilities, such as numerical reasoning.
- Personality questionnaires: also standardised, but measuring personality characteristics.
- Presentation exercises: where you are asked to present on a given topic to assessors.
- Analysis exercises: structured exercises where you are given particular scenarios or problems to work through under timed conditions.

Summary

We have begun the week with a general overview about what an Assessment Centre is. We have looked at its history, reasons for its popularity, what employers are often looking for in terms of 'Competencies', and the types of exercises that you are likely to encounter.

The following days of the week will focus on the individual exercises you are most likely to encounter in the Assessment Centres that you attend. These will include plenty of suggestions to ensure that you give your best on the day and avoid some common pitfalls.

You have taken the first key step to preparing yourself for an Assessment Centre. Preparation is invaluable to performing well at an Assessment Centre. You are already on the path to success!

Preparing for interviews

Introduction to the interview

As discussed on Sunday, Assessment Centres consist of a number of different exercises and events. An integral part of an Assessment Centre, however, is still the interview. Why is this, when employers have so many other exercises to choose from?

Interviews retain their importance, both in Assessment Centres and elsewhere as a recruitment tool, because:

- They are an effective information gathering tool for the recruiting organisation when conducted professionally
- They are also an important information gathering tool for you
- For both a potential employer and employee, an interview fulfills that very human need to meet each other and communicate face to face

An opportunity, not a threat

The interview, then, is your opportunity to display your relevant experience and Competencies. It is also an opportunity for you to find out what you need to know about the organisation and the role. However, interviews can often create anxiety. Perhaps this is because they come in so many different shapes and forms, and you may not know which style you will be facing until it begins.

The style of interviews can vary considerably in terms of the degree of formality adopted. Some interviews seem to have a less formal flavour, taking place around a low table or when interviewers and interviewees are seated in easy chairs. Others may seem more intimidating, with the interviewers sitting on the other side of a desk, and with a generally more formal setting. Even the number of interviews and interviewers can vary.

In addition, during the same interview, you will find that the style of questions frequently changes. Some questions 'open up' a particular topic (e.g. 'What did you enjoy most about that role?'). Other questions are more searching and ask for further elaboration or detail on a topic (e.g. 'Tell me more about that'). Finally, some questions seek specific clarification of details and facts (e.g. 'When exactly did you leave that role?').

Comments frequently heard from interviewees are:

'I got asked to give an example and my mind went blank.'

'When the time came for me to ask my questions I felt I let myself down.'

'When I was asked to initially "paint a picture of myself", I felt I could have given a better first impression'.

It need not be like this. Preparation combined with a sound interview technique on the day will turn your interview experience from something to be endured into a real opportunity to shine.

To begin this day of the week, let's look in turn at:

- The questions you are likely to face and top tips to help you prepare
- Questions you can ask to get the information you need, and at the same time create a positive impression
- Finally, your general interview technique which pulls it all together

Questions you are likely to face and top tips on how you can prepare

What we will look at now is the different types of questions you are likely to be asked in an interview within an Assessment Centre, and how you can prepare for them and make the most of the opportunities they present.

Preparation for the different types of questions will be critical to your success. These different types of questions can be summarised as follows:

- Questions about your career track record and experience
- Questions about Competencies relevant to the role

Questions about your career track record and experience

These questions look at the length and nature of your work experience. In particular, interviewers will be keen to explore the positions that you have held, the responsibilities that you had, and the depth of your technical knowledge and expertise in key areas. They will also be looking to fully account for any apparent gaps or breaks in your career history.

Questions in this area can cover four themes:

1 Your career direction
These questions focus on your career path to date and where you would like it to go. Typical questions include:

'Tell me a bit about yourself.'

'Where do you see your career heading?'

'What were you doing between (a particular gap in your employment record)?'

'What attracted you to that role?'

'Why did you leave the previous role?'

Top tips
Plan your responses to these and related questions about where you have come from and where you want to go in your career.

Pay particular attention in your preparation to your important 'lifeline junctions', such as career changes, and to any employment breaks – particularly in the last 10 years.

However, career paths, like train journeys, do not always proceed smoothly. At times they do not go as planned and to schedule! The key is to talk comfortably about the choices you have made, and the lessons and skills you have learned, and the positive aspects of the experience.

In preparation for a question along the lines of 'Tell me about yourself?', have in your mind a *short* (maximum 2 minutes) summary of yourself, covering your key experiences, key strengths, and the main reason why you are applying for the role, identifying how it fits in with your overall career goals.

2 Positions and responsibilities you have held
These questions focus more specifically on the positions themselves and their responsibilities. They will tend to focus on your more recent roles, but an earlier position may be explored more fully if it is felt to be particularly relevant to the job in question. Typical questions include:

'What were your main responsibilities in that role?'

'What was the purpose of the role?'

'Who did you report to?'

'What were you accountable for?'

Top tips
Plan your responses to these questions, particularly for your last three roles or for the last 10 years (whichever is the shorter). Differentiate clearly between the purpose of the job (why it existed) and the tasks you did.

3 Your technical knowledge and skills
These questions focus on the depth of your technical knowledge and skills in relevant areas. For example, an Office Manager may require technical knowledge about Microsoft Office and a Personnel Manager will be expected to have knowledge of employment legislation. Typical questions include:

'What are your technical strengths and limitations?'

'How do you keep your technical knowledge up to date?'

'What professional publications do you read on a regular basis?'

'What would you see as the key technical demands of this role?'

Top tips
Plan your responses to these questions. Be clear about your areas of strength and how you can tackle / are tackling any areas where you are not as strong.

If appropriate, ensure that your professional memberships are up to date and keep yourself abreast of any relevant stories in newspapers / journals relating to technical products / processes in your areas of relevant expertise.

4 *Your achievements and successes*

These questions focus on your key achievements to date and the particular successes that you have had in relevant areas. It is less about the roles you have held and the tasks you performed (which are covered in questions about your position and responsibilities), but more about how successfully you did it and what you achieved.

It is worth noting that candidates often sell themselves short in this area. This is a pity, because employers are looking for people who can replicate their previous successes in a new setting. Typical questions include:

'What are your key achievements to date?'

'What were your main successes in that role?'

'What challenges did you face in the role of . . . ?'

Top tips:
Plan your responses to these questions, and in particular try to have at least *two* achievements for your last *two* roles clear in your mind.

Focus on *your* achievements: avoid the royal 'we'!

Make your achievements as relevant as you can to the role you are applying for.

Be specific if you can, and quantify your achievements as much as possible, for example:

'I improved the company's financial performance by 10 per cent.'

'I reduced staff turnover by 20 per cent.'

'I was sales representative of the year.'

'I successfully passed my professional exams whilst studying part-time over those 2 years.'

Make sure your achievements are justifiable, because you are likely to have further questions on them during the interview. Your achievements may also be verified with your referees.

Questions about Competencies

These questions look at when you have demonstrated the required Competencies in the past. As discussed yesterday, a

Competency – such as 'Planning and organising' – is a clearly defined grouping of qualities which is required to perform a job effectively.

When assessing your Competencies, interviewers are still working on the premise that the best gauge of future performance is past performance. However, the focus here is very much on 'how' people have done things (the Competencies they used and clearly demonstrated) rather than 'what' they necessarily achieved.

Competency questions will vary, but they often follow a particular pattern that you can use to good effect to help your preparation. Have a look at the example question below for the Competency of Planning and organising:

Opening question
'Talk us through an example of when you planned a particular project . . .'

Follow-up question 1
'What was the situation?'

Follow-up question 2
'What tasks had to be done?'

Follow-up question 3
'What actions did you take to plan the project?'

Follow-up question 4
'What was the result?'

Top tips
As you can see, a Competency-based interview question asks you to describe a particular example or event. You are then

often asked a series of follow-up questions to expand on the situation, what you did and what the outcome was.

Candidates who have not had the opportunity to prepare can often find these questions very demanding. This is because you are having to talk through real events and in some detail. Preparation really pays dividends in this area.

The preparation you will need to do for any Competency interview is to consider firstly what likely Competencies are required for the role. If possible, try to get the Competencies, or at least information indicating what they are likely to be, from the employer (such as the Person/Job Specification). If you cannot do this, don't worry, use our Competency definitions in Appendix 1 to inform your choice and predictions.

Not all the Competencies in Appendix 1 will be relevant for every role. Look to identify the ones which you feel would be the most important. Work on around a maximum of nine for any one role.

Having identified the Competencies, plan your preparation using the acronym STAR:

- **S** is the **Situation** that sets the scene for the particular Competency – this needs to be a real life example that you experienced personally
- **T** is the **Tasks** that needed to be undertaken to resolve the situation or problem represented above
- **A** is the **Action** or activity clearly taken, by you, in response to the situation
- **R** is the **Result** – think of it as the happy ending arising from the Actions you demonstrated above!

As you can see, this acronym mirrors the follow-up questions asked in the earlier example.

In Appendix 2, you will find a template that you can use for each Competency that you prepare.

Ideally, draw upon a mix of recent examples (preferably from approximately the last 2–3 years, because these are easier to recall in detail) that cover different situations from your career to date. Also, feel free to include noteworthy examples from outside of work.

In the interview itself, listen carefully to the phrasing of the exact question that you are given. Clarify the question if you are unsure, and take your time before answering.

Be concise and focused – try to use no more than a couple of sentences on each STAR element. Remember to describe what you did rather than what the team did – do not fall into the trap of being too modest!

A good way to practice this is either to talk through your evidence with a friend, record it on tape or talk to yourself in a mirror. We suggest you do the latter in a private rather than public place! The key is to become comfortable when articulating your examples.

Questions you can ask

It is important during the interview, and during other appropriate opportunities in the Assessment Centre, that you ask questions that you really want answered – rather than just asking questions for the sake of it.

Preparing your questions
It is critical that you make the most of your time before the Assessment Centre to gather as much information as you can about the organisation and the role. This will prove invaluable in helping you prepare for the selection process, as well as deciding if the role is right for you. Useful sources of information are:

- Company brochures such as annual accounts, sales materials etc.
- Job-related information, for example: a Job Description and Person Specification
- Personal networking – that is, speaking to people who know about the organisation – for instance, existing and past employees
- The organisation's website
- Other information gathering websites such as www.ft.com; www.kompass.com; and www.hoovers.com. Internet sites are useful in

providing information not just on the organisation, but on its position in the marketplace – including who its competitors are

The interview itself

The interview is an opportunity for you to find out more about the company and role. You need to be able to answer the following questions by the time you leave the Assessment Centre:

'Would I want to work for this organisation?'

'Can I do this role and would I want to do it?'

'How will this role help me to achieve my broader career goals?'

Working on this premise, ensure that you focus on the key questions. The list below covers a selection of likely question topics for your information gathering:

- The purpose of the role – why does the post exist?
- The key responsibilities of the role and main tasks to be performed
- The resources available to the post holder, such as budget, staff etc.
- The team and department within which the role resides – structure and size
- The reason why the role is vacant – is it a new role or an existing role?
- The 'culture' of the organisation, that is, the 'atmosphere' within the organisation; the way things are done; the values of the organisation
- The future plans of the organisation – its priorities for the current year, and where it sees itself in 3 years

> • What training and development opportunities are in
>   place to help staff develop within the organisation?

The other useful question to ask at the end of any interview is:

> • What is the next stage in the selection process –
>   when will a decision be made?

General interview technique

As we said earlier, your general interview technique ensures
that you present your career track record, experience and
Competencies in the best light.

Top tips
The acronym **FABULOUS** summarises our top tips for your
interview technique:

F is for First impressions
As with any initial meeting, it is particularly important to
make a positive first impression. Both at the beginning and
end of the interview session, shake hands firmly, but not so
firmly that you cause injury to the interviewer!

When meeting the interviewer(s) for the first time, project
warmth and interest by making eye contact and smiling as
you introduce yourself.

While business formality over the last 10 years has relaxed, it
is still advisable to address the interviewer(s) by their
surname – unless they address you first by your first name,
and specifically invite you to call them by their first names.

Have your 'antenna raised' when you first meet the interviewer(s) – be aware of their style (how formal is the language used, mannerisms etc.?) and adjust your style (if you can) to match theirs.

A is for Appearance
Be conscious of your personal grooming and ensure that you are projecting the impression that you would like to make.

As an aid to help you relax, you may find it advisable to avoid wearing brand new clothing: instead, choose a smart suit or outfit that you feel comfortable in. As a rule of thumb, if in doubt about the dress code, always err on the conservative side (e.g. suits or outfits of a darker colour).

B is for Body language
Your voice: vary your pitch, pace and tone to make your communication more interesting to the audience. If you are naturally quietly spoken, try to raise your voice more, but avoid shouting! If you know that you talk more quickly when you are anxious, slow your delivery down and build in time to breathe!

Your posture: your posture should communicate your attentiveness and interest. Sit up straight, but not uncomfortably so. Fold your hands comfortably in front of you, but ensure that you make full use of hand movements to emphasise points without undue exaggeration.

Your eye contact: make eye contact with the interviewer, but ensure that this is not continuous! Where there is more than one interviewer, ensure that you have the most eye contact with the person who asks the question. Then, between questions, make some eye contact with all the other interviewers.

U is for Use your time well
It is important not to over-answer questions. Keep your replies focused on the question and aim for a maximum 2-minute reply per question. The interviewer(s) will ask if they require more information.

L is for Looking and listening
Look out for any mannerisms or signals from the interviewer(s) that your answers may be going on for too long or too short a period. If in doubt, do not be afraid to ask, 'Am I covering the right ground here for you?'

Listen carefully to the interview questions. Furthermore, communicate to the interviewer(s) that you are listening by looking attentive, nodding and making eye contact. If you are unclear at any time about a question, ask them to repeat the question or to expand upon it. Never respond to what you think you have been asked – always respond to what you know you have been asked.

O is for Offer
Talk about what you can offer the organisation, but do not raise the topic about what salary might be on offer to you.

However, if the issue of salary is raised by the interviewer(s), ensure that you know the market range for the role and state that you would be looking for something within that range.

An Assessment Centre interview will not normally be the place for you to engage in salary negotiation. Instead, your focus is to ensure that the employer fully sees your capabilities and how you can benefit the organisation. Salary discussions are more appropriate – and more likely to go in your favour – once a tangible offer of employment is on the cards.

U is for 'Up-for-the-job'

It is important to communicate your enthusiasm for the role to the interviewers. They need to feel that you can both do the job, and that you want it.

It is equally critical that you not only know your strengths and achievements, but that you can project them with confidence during the interview.

'Projection' can be developed. Look at the characteristics you see others display when they are confident, and practice using them yourself in your preparation of interview replies. As mentioned earlier, your practice could include 'role-play' with a friend, talking into a tape recorder or talking into a mirror.

WARNING

Do not criticise previous managers, colleagues or employers during the interview. Also, avoid being negative about any aspects of your career history to date, for instance being made redundant or a career move.

S is for Strengths

Know your key achievements and strengths – in particular, those that you have identified as relevant to the role. Also, be aware of your limitations and be prepared to share them if asked – ensure that you present them in a 'balanced' manner. Acknowledge how you are addressing your limitations, as well as how they can also be seen as a strength, for example, 'Sometimes I may ask too much of others in my desire to reach targets and get results'.

Summary

Today we have covered the style of interview that you are likely to encounter within an Assessment Centre. Specifically, we have looked at the types of questions you will be asked, questions for you to ask, and getting the best out of the interview using the **FABULOUS** top tips.

Preparing for group exercises

Introduction to Group Exercises

Another important and often used element within an
Assessment Centre is the Group Exercise. By a Group
Exercise, we mean:

- You are one of a number of individuals working
  together as a group
- A task is given to the 'group' to complete, often
  under timed conditions
- Assessors are present to observe: whether the
  group completes the task; how the group
  approaches the task; and your individual contribution
  in relation to the Competencies

Group Exercises have been used ever since Assessment
Centres came on the scene and they fall into a category of
exercises called 'simulation exercises'.

A 'simulation exercise' is different to an interview. In an interview, it is ultimately about you saying what skills you can offer, or talking about what motivates you, and so on. A Group Exercise is about what you do in a 'live' setting. A Group Exercise gives an opportunity for the assessors to observe you 'in action' – what you say, how you react to the task and, indeed, to the other candidates.

Typical Competencies assessed by Group Exercises

The evidence that the assessors collect from the Group Exercise is as likely to come from your approach to the task, as from whether you complete it.

Remember from Sunday that exact Competency definitions will vary from organisation to organisation and from role to role. The more you can find out about the Competencies the better. However, the following Competencies are more likely to be assessed during Group Exercises.

- **Leadership**
- **Relating to others**
- **Persuasive communications**
- **Self-motivation and resilience**

For each of these four Competencies, refer to the fuller descriptions in Appendix 1. Think also about how you could make the most of your strengths in a Group Exercise.

Different types of Group Exercises

Broadly speaking, Group Exercises fall into two categories:

- *Discussion based*: where the group is asked to debate and often reach consensus and conclusions on a topic or on topics.
- *Practical tasks*: where the group is asked to design and physically construct something.

Discussion based

Discussion-based Group Exercises are the most commonly used type in an Assessment Centre.

Individuals tend to be seated around a table in a group size of between four to six. There will tend to be two to three assessors in the room, set back from the group.

Depending on the seniority of the role, Group Exercises will tend to last between 30–90 minutes. However, not all of that time will be taken up with discussion. It may include time for individuals to review the materials before the discussion formally begins.

The actual topic(s) may be completely unrelated to the work setting. For example, you may be asked to assume that you are all in a hot air balloon that is slowly losing height over the ocean. The group has to agree which items they need to discard, and in what order, so that height can be maintained until landfall is reached. At the other end of the scale, the topics will be work related and tailored specifically to the role being assessed. Here you are likely to find more complex briefing materials.

You may find that you and each of the other candidates are given different briefing materials or asked to play a particular role in the discussion (e.g. someone is representing Finance, someone else Marketing etc.).

The topics may have no simple – or indeed single – answer and the candidates have to reach a consensus on the course of action.

Practical tasks
Practical task Group Exercises, though less widely used, do still occur in Assessment Centres. These types of exercises have moved on considerably from their military origins. The military made use of planks of wood, oil drums and ropes and still do!

The principle underpinning the use of the practical task, however, remains the same. Their purpose is to place all candidates on an even footing by reducing the advantages of prior job knowledge and experience. The types of practical tasks that you are more likely to face in today's Assessment Centres are indoor exercises involving equipment such as:

- Table-top plastic construction kits (often using K'nex and Lego style materials)
- Larger versions of the above requiring a reasonable amount of floor space for design and construction activities

The task will often require you to design and construct a particular object (car, bridge, chair etc.) within certain time and material constraints.

Common concerns and top tips

Common concerns specific to Group Exercises are captured by the following questions:

How can I prepare beforehand?

As with interview preparation, try to find out the exact Competency definitions used by the recruiting organisation. These will give a steer on the type of style required for effective performance in the role. If you cannot, do not worry – use the Competency definitions in Appendix 1.

For each of the Competencies, reflect upon your strengths and your developmental 'blind spots' (which we all have) – particularly those which might show when you are in meetings and when working with others.

For example, you are aware that you could do more to acknowledge the contributions of others in your day-to-day working. Write a short action plan of things to do more of when you are undertaking the Group Exercise. By doing this, you will see benefit, not just at an Assessment Centre, but on a day-to-day basis.

If you are in a Group Exercise where individual preparation time has been allocated, allow yourself sufficient time to familiarise yourself with all the materials. Ensure that you have reviewed all of the material by the end of the allocated time, even if this is just at a 'surface' level.

How should I act?

The key tip here is – do not act. You will find it difficult to sustain a role for the duration of a Group Exercise, let alone for the whole Assessment Centre. Rather, be yourself and work on making the most of your strengths and showing them to best effect on the day.

What are the common pitfalls to avoid?

It is easy in a Group Exercise to forget about the common courtesies that we would all expect to see displayed in group situations.

Do:

- Address others by their names
- Invite others to contribute – particularly those who seem reticent or quiet
- Listen to others; actively acknowledge their contributions
- Be clear on what the task is before you start, and try your best to complete it
- Throw yourself in to the task and contribute fully
- Accept the constraints placed on you by the exercise instructions
- Check the resources available to you – these may be physical things like a flip chart, a computer and calculators
- Be prepared to respond positively and appropriately to any unexpected changes that the assessors make to the exercise brief

Do not:

- Interrupt others
- Become aggressive or argumentative
- Monopolise the 'airtime'
- Be frightened to ask questions of assessors and fellow participants
- Forget to monitor the time
- Be put off by the presence of the assessors – once the exercise begins, most people soon forget they are there

How should I behave with the other candidates?

Remember you are working as a team to complete the task. Do not try to score 'points' against the other candidates.

Should I become the Timekeeper, the Note-taker or 'the Person at the flip chart'?

Some candidates jump in very quickly to adopt these roles. If you feel comfortable performing any of these roles, that is fine – but ensure the roles do not get in the way of allowing you to contribute in other ways.

How do I tackle a very dominant candidate?

Very dominant candidates are unlikely to be doing themselves a service by behaving in this way. If leadership is being assessed, it tends to be defined in more consultative or collaborative terms these days. Useful questions to manage the situation include:

'Shall we see what others think about this approach before we rush in . . .?'

'Can we just check we are all happy with this?'

However, it is critical that your voice is heard – and this is not about shouting! Politely stand your ground and, if you are talked over, be prepared to repeat your point.

What do I do if one candidate is extremely quiet?

When working as a group, it is important to ensure that all members of the group contribute. If you aware that a candidate is very quiet, ask an open question like, 'What do we all think about this?' If the individual does not take up this opportunity, a little later address them by name as follows, '(first name), what are your thoughts?'

I have heard that sometimes the instructions change half-way through. What do I do?

You may encounter changes to the exercise remit – in just the same way that the goalposts change in all the jobs we have. These changes can take the form of extra information, changes to the instructions, changes of time-scale and so on. The key is not to complain and not to challenge them! Just go with the flow. Ask aloud, 'Based on this development, what changes do we need to make?'

If I am assigned a specific role in a group discussion exercise, what should I do?

As mentioned earlier, you could be given a specific role to play in a group discussion that would include having reference materials unique to you. A key point is to accept the role and any constraints placed upon you – remember that the other candidates will have to do exactly the same.

Look to strike a balance between being true to yourself, and incorporating the approach required by someone performing the role. For example, if your role was to act as the company accountant in the Group Exercise, try to convey the importance of financial considerations in the subsequent discussion.

Are there any particular tips for practical exercises?

All the tips given above apply to both practical and discussion-based exercises, but there are two extra considerations:

1 Make sure that you are wearing smart but practical clothing appropriate to the exercise. Assessors will often notify you in advance if they are planning to run a practical exercise. Dress code for practical exercises tends to be less formal, reflecting the need to work with physical materials on the floor and to 'roll up your sleeves'.
2 The issue of special requirements will be covered in more detail on Saturday. It is worth stressing here the importance of making the assessors aware of any special requirements specific to an exercise of a more practical nature (e.g. mobility).

Summary

Today we have looked at Group Exercises. Specifically, we have discussed the type of exercises you are likely to encounter and top tips to help you during this important element of an Assessment Centre.

Preparing for psychometric tests and questionnaires

Introduction to psychometric assessment

Psychometric assessment often plays an important part in an Assessment Centre – but for candidates, it is often one of the most dreaded parts of the day. For many, even the term itself smacks of some unpleasant psychological scrutiny and gives rise to feelings of worry about what the exercises might unearth. Today we will 'demystify' the process for you and give you some top tips to ensure that you do yourself justice on the day.

Definition

So what does the term 'Psychometrics' actually mean? It is literally 'measurement of the mind'. In reality, it means measuring a broad range of characteristics, skills, abilities and behaviours governed by our mind.

From your perspective, it is important to differentiate between the two broad types of psychometric instruments that you are likely to encounter within the context of an Assessment Centre, namely tests and questionnaires.

- *Tests* have right and wrong answers (as do educational exams). This is because they are looking at specific skills and abilities.

- *Questionnaires* do not have right or wrong answers. Instead they look at how you describe your style, interests or motivation, and how this picture of yourself relates to the requirements of the job and the organisation.

Background

Psychometrics is not a new science. The first commercially available tests were published in the early part of the last century. Particular growth periods occurred during the two world wars, when psychometric assessment significantly assisted with matching the large volume of individuals to different roles within the military, as well as identifying Officer potential.

Their popularity grew rapidly in the post-war years, as employers increasingly saw the benefits that well-designed and professionally administered and interpreted tests and questionnaires brought to their recruitment processes, namely:

- Consistent and dependable results through careful standardisation of the way the exercises are administered and used (candidates who have been through tests and questionnaires in recent years often comment upon the classroom style in which the exercises are sat)
- The objectivity of test or questionnaire results
- The accuracy with which tests or questionnaires predict specific characteristics and skills in the workplace

Range of tests and questionnaires

It may come as a surprise to know that there are several thousand commercially available psychometric tests and questionnaires in the UK. Some of these are for use in non-work settings, such as clinical and educational applications. Even if we focus solely on those tests and questionnaires designed specifically for use in the workplace, we are still left with several hundred commercially available products.

However, as an individual applying for a graduate, professional or managerial role at an Assessment Centre, the reality is that you are most likely to encounter the following:

- Ability Tests
- Personality Questionnaires

As mentioned on Sunday, Assessment Centre formats vary, and you may be asked to complete several tests or questionnaires drawn from the above areas. Alternatively, you may not have to complete any!

Today we will focus upon these two categories of exercises and provide you with examples of each to aid your understanding and preparation.

Different ways to complete tests and questionnaires

This has been an area of significant development since the early 1990s. There are now three main ways of completing psychometric tests and questionnaires:

- Online – via the internet
- On-screen – via desktop PCs/laptops and also by using hand-held technology such as pocket PCs
- Paper and pencil – under the supervision of a trained Test Administrator in a 'classroom' style setting

Ability Tests

Ability Tests can be either tests of a general nature which look to measure 'general intelligence', or they can focus on specific abilities such as verbal ability and numerical ability.

There are many different types of tests available in each category; the exact type that you may encounter will depend on the specific level of job you are applying for – some tests are pitched specifically at very senior levels.

For the rest of today we will focus on 'specific Ability Tests' as these are more commonly used within Assessment Centres. There are many Ability Tests available which cover a wide range of verbal, numerical, abstract, spatial and mechanical abilities. However, for the majority of graduate, professional and managerial vacancies, the Ability Tests that you are more likely to encounter are abstract, verbal and numerical reasoning.

In these three areas a typical test would tend to take between 25–45 minutes. Examples of these are shown below:

Graduate and Managerial Assessment

The GMA consists of three tests which cover Abstract, Verbal and Numerical Reasoning respectively.

There follows one example of each of these tests for you to gain a feel for the product.

Abstract reasoning

This is a test of your skill at finding similarities and differences in groups of patterns. All the patterns in group A are in some way similar to each other, and all those in group B are similar to each other.

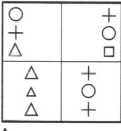
A

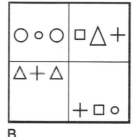
B

Below, you will find five separate boxes with patterns in them. Your task is to decide if each box:

i) belongs to group A
ii) belongs to group B
iii) belongs to neither group

Answers:

first is group A
second is group B
third is neither group
fourth is neither group
fifth is group A

Verbal reasoning

This is a test of your skill at making sense of reports which cannot be relied on to be objective, truthful or even consistent. The test consists of a series of short passages, each of which includes a number of short statements intended to convey information or persuade the reader of a point of view.

Each passage is accompanied by four statements relating to the information or arguments it contains. Assume that what is stated is true; even if it contradicts what you know or believe to be the case in reality. Decide on this assumption whether the statement is:

a) true,
b) false,
c) you cannot tell and need more information.

In recent years it has become clear that man's use of fossil fuels is likely to have a major impact on the world's climate. As a result of this, increased concentrations of 'greenhouse' gasses such as carbon dioxide and methane will lead to global warming; an overall small increase in average temperatures; whose impact is difficult to predict.

Whilst some scientists predict melting of the polar icecaps, and so a rise in sea levels, others think this will be balanced by increased precipitation at the poles.

1 If we go on using fossil fuels at the present rate, we must expect climatic change.
   TRUE : FALSE : CAN'T TELL

2 Depletion of the ozone layer will result in global warming.
   TRUE : FALSE : ***CAN'T TELL***

3 Scientists are all agreed that use of fossil fuels will eventually lead to a rise in sea levels.
   TRUE : ***FALSE*** : CAN'T TELL

4 The burning of fossil fuels increases the concentration of methane in the atmosphere.
   TRUE : FALSE : CAN'T TELL

Numerical reasoning

This is a test of your skill at reasoning with numbers. First you are given some information in a variety of forms – text, tables or graphs – followed by three related questions. For each question, choose what you think is the correct answer from the possible answers A to P.

An insurance scheme pays benefits to its members who are sick for extended periods of time at the following rates

1st month:	nil
2nd–4th months:	50% of normal salary
5th and succeeding months:	25% of normal salary

on the first £24,000 p.a. of salary for each month in which the member is sick and is not paid by the employer. How much does the scheme pay to:

1 John, who is off work for two months, whose salary is £12,000 p.a., and who gets no sick pay?

2 Pat, who is ill for six months, but who is paid normally for the first two months and whose salary is £18,000 p.a.?

3 Hilary, whose salary is £30,000 p.a., who gets 3 months sick pay from her employer, and who has to take nine months off?

A) £250	B) £500	C) £750	D) £1000
E) £1125	F) £1500	G) £1765	H) £2125
I) £2250	J) £2350	K) £2500	L) £3125
M) £3750	N) £4000	O) £5000	P) £5625

Answers:

1 Answer B is correct. John gets £500.00 (1 month at half his usual monthly salary)

2 Answer I is correct. Pat gets £2250 (3 months at half her usual monthly salary)

3 Answer N is correct. Hilary gets £4000 (3 months at half of a monthly salary of £2,000 plus 2 months at a quarter of a monthly salary of £2,000)

GMA – A Test Taker's Guide © 1992 S.F. Blinkhorn. Reproduced with permission of the publishers, ASE, Chiswick Centre, 414 Chiswick High Road, London W4 5TF a division of nfer Nelson, Tel +44(0) 208 996 3337. Email contact@ase-solutions.co.uk. Website www.ase-solutions.co.uk

Personality Questionnaires

Personality Questionnaires look at your typical 'style' of behaviour and not your ability. In other words, how you prefer to do things typically, such as the way you relate to others or how you approach tasks and solve problems.

A Personality Questionnaire is essentially a structured form of self-assessment and it tends to be completed without any time constraints.

There are a number of well-established work-based Personality Questionnaires used in the UK. Personality characteristics that are normally assessed include social confidence, anxiety levels and preferences for making speedy decisions. Questionnaires will vary in the number of personality characteristics that they look to measure – some will measure 5, some 16, and some 32.

Personality Questionnaires will also have different ways of asking their questions. Examples of two common styles of question format are shown below:

Personality Questionnaires

Here are some examples of the types of questions that might be asked.

1 Rating Statements

In this example you are asked to rate yourself on a number of phrases or statements. After reading each statement mark your answer according to the following rules:

Fill in circle 1	If you strongly disagree with the statement
Fill in circle 2	If you disagree with the statement
Fill in circle 3	If you are unsure
Fill in circle 4	If you agree with the statement
Fill in circle 5	If you strongly agree with the statement

The first statement has already been completed for you. The person has agreed that 'I enjoy meeting new people' is an accurate description of him/herself.

Now try questions 2 to 6 for yourself by completely filling in the circle that is most true for you.

	Strongly disagree	Disagree	Unsure	Agree	Strongly agree
1 I enjoy meeting new people	①	②	③	●	⑤
2 I like helping people	①	②	③	④	⑤
3 I sometimes make mistakes	①	②	③	④	⑤
4 I don't mind taking risks	①	②	③	④	⑤
5 I'm easily disappointed	①	②	③	④	⑤
6 I enjoy repairing things	①	②	③	④	⑤

2 Making Choices

In this example you are given a block of four statements: A, B, C and D. Your task is to choose the statement which you think is most true or typical of you in your everyday behaviour and then choose the one which is least true or typical of you. Indicate your choices by filling in the appropriate circle in the row marked 'M' (for Most) and in the next row 'L' (for Least).

The first block has been completed for you. The person has chosen, 'Enjoys organising people' as most true (or typical) and 'Seeks variety' as being least true (or typical) of him/herself. Now try questions 2, 3 and 4 yourself.

I am the sort of person who . . .

1 A Has a wide circle of friends
   B Enjoys organising people
   C Relaxes easily
   D Seeks variety

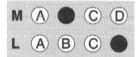

2 A Helps people with their problems
   B Develops new approaches
   C Has lots of energy
   D Enjoys social activities

3 A Has lots of new ideas
   B Feels calm
   C Likes to understand things
   D Is easy to get on with

4 A Enjoys organising events
  B Sometimes gets angry
  C Is talkative
  D Resolves conflicts at work

© SHL Group plc

How your results are interpreted

So how are your results interpreted from tests and questionnaires? The key principle with both tests and questionnaires is that they do not look only at how you completed the assessment, but at how your score compares to a large sample of people who have taken the assessment previously.

Imagine that you have just completed a Personality Questionnaire at an Assessment Centre. Your responses to the questions are then compared to the responses of a group of people who took the questionnaire previously, for example, 'UK Managers and Professionals'. This will give an indication of how strong your preferences/characteristics are relative to that group, and what this is likely to mean in terms of how you 'behave'.

With Ability Tests, the principle remains the same. The organisation is interested in relating your test performance to individuals of a relevant background for the role in question – do you perform in the top 25 per cent, the bottom 25 per cent, or is your performance typical of most managers?

Common concerns and top tips

What can I do beforehand to help me with tests?

Once advised that you will be completing an Ability Test, ask if you will be sent practice leaflets. If specific practice leaflets are not available, useful websites that provide a selection of online practice questions and information are:

www.shlgroup.com/candidate/default.htm

www.ase-solutions.co.uk/support.asp?id=63

Do yourself justice by practising the relevant skill areas. For example, in order to brush up on your numerical reasoning skills, read financial reports in newspapers, practise studying and interpreting information presented in a numerical format, and refresh your memory about straightforward calculations, such as percentages.

Finally, if you are going to complete a numerical test, take your own calculator. If you are allowed to use calculators, it will normally be acceptable for you to use your own.

What can I do beforehand to help me with questionnaires?

Fairly limited, but once advised that you will be completing a Personality Questionnaire, ask if you will be sent a practice leaflet or any further information on the questionnaire.

What should I remember if I am completing a questionnaire online?

If you are completing the questionnaire over the internet, ensure that you give yourself quality time for its completion, i.e. sufficient time, and time free from distractions or interruptions.

In addition, if you have been asked to complete more than one questionnaire, consider taking a break between each questionnaire.

What can I do during the session to help me with tests?

Listen carefully to the instructions. Do not be afraid to ask questions – the other candidates are likely to be thinking the same! Make the most of any practice questions; they are there to help you and to prompt questions from you. Read each question carefully before answering.

Unless instructed otherwise, if you are unsure of an answer, mark your best choice, then move on to the next question. You may not necessarily be expected to fully complete all the questions in the test. Work quickly, but not so quickly that your accuracy is potentially undermined. Most of the tests will be timed, therefore, monitor your time.

I have special requirements. What should I do?

If you have any special requirements, contact the organisation. If you wear glasses, contact lenses, hearing aids etc., ensure you take them with you.

What can I do during the session to help me with questionnaires?

With most questionnaires, you are asked to consider how you typically behave in a work setting. If this is the case, think about yourself in a work rather than home or leisure setting.

Work through the questions at a comfortable pace, but do not ponder too long over any one question. The questionnaire is about how you see yourself now, so ensure that your self-assessment is up to date!

Do not try to create an 'unreal' image; be honest about how you see yourself rather than presenting how you would like to be.

How can I find out more?

Go to the websites listed earlier, or consult the Further Reading section at the back of this book. Moreover, if you have been to an Assessment Centre that involves completing tests and questionnaires – ask for feedback. This will help you to find out more about the process, as well as about yourself!

Summary

Today we have discussed psychometric assessment. We have looked at the more widely-used psychometric tests and questionnaires that you may encounter, and given examples of the more common formats. We have provided top tips to help you before and during the assessment sessions.

Preparing for Presentation Exercises

Introduction to Presentation Exercises

Candidates are often asked to give a presentation in an Assessment Centre. The presentation element has a number of distinct phases, each of which requires a particular approach to get the best out of the exercise. Today we will look in more detail at each of these phases and the issues you need to consider. For each phase we will give you top tips to ensure that your presentation will be a success.

The phases

- *Preparation for the presentation, in response to the topic you have been given*: the topic may be given to you a number of days before the Assessment Centre is due to take place. Alternatively, you may not be given the topic until the very day of the Assessment Centre, and in these circumstances clearly your preparation time is going to be far more limited.
- *Delivering an effective presentation*: your presentation may be delivered to any number of assessors, from just one person to a very large audience. Sometimes the other candidates at the Assessment Centre are also invited to listen to your presentation and sit with the assessors. A more commonly adopted approach is that your presentation (and subsequent 'questions and answers') is delivered to a small panel of assessors, who then immediately follow the presentation with an interview.

- *Dealing with any questions from the audience arising from your presentation*: often the panel has set aside a number of minutes for the specific purpose of asking you questions about the presentation you have made.

Of course, assessors are often particularly interested in presentation performance when the post itself requires the job-holder to make presentations in the course of their duties, for example, a Sales Manager having to make sales pitches.

Candidates often find making presentations very stressful, particularly when the success (or otherwise) of their application depends upon it. Even experienced presenters rarely fully overcome their nerves – and some argue that nerves in moderation can be a good thing to keep you 'on your toes'.

As with other elements of an Assessment Centre, the key is to be familiar with how presentations are assessed and, through a combination of preparation, practice, and some useful practical hints, to ensure that you do yourself justice on the day.

An effective presentation is rather like being on the stage. For a few minutes you have complete control of the audience. They are, literally, all ears, waiting on your every word.

Take heart – even if public speaking concerns you, presentation performance can be massively improved by preparation and the application of just a few key tactics.

Typical Competencies assessed by Presentation Exercises

As you know from Sunday, the goal in any assessment process is to provide an opportunity for candidates to display the relevant Competencies. You will remember that exact Competency definitions will vary from organisation to organisation and from role to role. The more you can find out about the Competencies, the better. Below are some Competencies that will tend to be assessed during Presentation Exercises.

The assessment will be based around how you delivered your presentation; how you dealt with subsequent questions from the assessors; and, depending upon how technical the topic is, what you said.

- **Planning and organising**
- **Persuasive communications**
- **Self-motivation and resilience**

For each of these three Competencies, refer to the fuller descriptions in Appendix 1. Think also about how you could make the most of your strengths in a Presentation Exercise.

WARNING

The above Competencies (or something very similar, depending upon the organisation's precise definition) will tend to be assessed regardless of the exact topic of the Presentation. Other Competencies may or may not be assessed depending upon how 'technical' the topic is.

Different types of topic

By 'technical' topics, we mean whether the topic you have been given relates directly to knowledge and/or experience required in the role.

If 'non-technical', the topic may be of much less importance to the assessors, and the content of what you say is simply the means by which, for instance, your communication skills are assessed.

Sample 'non-technical' topics that you might be given could include:

- My finest moment
- My greatest achievement

Common concerns and top tips

Some of the most commonly asked questions and our top tips are shown below.

I have just been given the topic. How can I prepare beforehand?

As with interview and Group Exercise preparation, try to find out the exact Competency definitions used by the recruiting organisation. These will give a steer to the style required for effective performance in the role. If you cannot, do not worry – use the Competency definitions in Appendix 1.

If the topic is 'technical', look for clues in the Job Description and Person Specification to any important themes or issues that you might wish to cover in your presentation. Think about what other Competencies (maximum three) from our Appendix might be assessed, such as Analysing and solving problems.

Check the information that you have been given. Make sure that you know how long you have to present, and what resources are available to you in the form of an overhead projector, flip chart facility or a computer-based projector. If you are using the latter, and it is being supplied by the organisation, ensure that you know exactly what version and release of software you are going to be using on the day to avoid compatibility problems.

Look carefully at the topic you have been given. Check that you understand exactly what is being sought. Even if you think you do, check with a trusted friend or family member what they think the topic is all about. If anything requires clarification – contact the organisation.

Draft out the key points that you want to get across in your presentation, but pay careful attention to the time that you have been allocated. A common trap is to try to cover too much.

Think carefully too about the audience. Make sure that the content of your Presentation is pitched at the right tone and level for them.

Plan out how long you have until the presentation and how much time you will need to allow for your preparation, not forgetting things like preparing slides and hand-outs.

For a pre-prepared presentation, we recommend that you allow a ratio of *10 minutes' preparation time for each minute of delivery time*.

If you can – stop at this point in your preparation! Put your work away and go and do something different. Come back later and look again at the topic and your earlier work – you will be surprised how, in the intervening time, your brain has come up with some new or alternative ideas.

When you are comfortable with the content of your presentation, do a draft of your slides and hand-outs. Keep the slides simple – just headings covering key points. Aim for a maximum of one slide for each 45 seconds or one minute of delivery time – less if you are particularly confident at delivering presentations with minimal supporting materials.

Now, do a draft of what you are going to say, either written out on small index cards, or on the computer in note form – these are prompts for your eyes only. If you can, avoid putting too much detail down – you do not want to be seen simply reading off cards or notes in your presentation.

Make sure that the presentation has a proper introduction and a conclusion. Try to leave 'on a high' – make the last point upbeat and positive, and then recap on the whole content with a conclusion. A clear conclusion is particularly important – you *must* revisit the main points you have made.

Rehearse your presentation. Inflict it mercilessly on members of your family, a supportive friend, to yourself in a mirror, even to the pet cat or dog – they generally do not complain. The key, of course, is to feel relaxed and comfortable with the content. Remember to speak a little more slowly than normal to ensure that the audience has time to absorb the content.

Invite honest feedback – unless it is your pet (in our view, dogs tend to say everything is perfect and cats tend to be too critical). In particular, check how you fared against the time you have been given – was the presentation too long or short? Does the message clearly address the topic you were given? Was the language and tone you used relevant to the level of the audience?

Remember to make backups, particularly if you are using a computer-based projector. As a minimum you should have spare hard copies of any slides, notes and hand-outs that you are intending to use, as well as a backup disc.

I have been told I won't get the topic until the day of the Assessment Centre.

All the above principles apply, but our '10 to 1' rule may not be possible. You may not have much time to practise or the luxury of being able to leave your first draft workings and come back to them later. Instead, planning your preparation activity will become particularly critical.

As a rough guide, allow 60 per cent of your total preparation time to developing the content of what you want to say; 20 per cent to preparing slides/acetates; and 20 per cent to a final rehearsal and fine-tuning.

What about delivering the presentation itself?

Check that all the materials you need are to hand, and any technology you are about to use has been tested before you begin.

Make sure that you have a glass of water in case your voice gets dry.

Speak clearly, and a little more slowly than normal speaking speed. Use pauses effectively to emphasise key points and when moving on from one content area to another.

Vary your voice and pitch to give your delivery some richness and depth.

Speak loudly enough so that those in the back of the room can hear you adequately, though try not to shout.

Use hand movements effectively but sparingly to emphasise key points.

It is important to develop eye contact with the audience. Move your eyes over the entire audience, but do not linger too long over any one individual.

If you can, try to take a step or two occasionally from the podium or your 'base point' towards the audience. This can be a very powerful way of retaining audience attention, particularly if you time it to coincide with an important point in your presentation. In these instances, it helps to have index card notes so that you are not too tied to the computer for your prompts.

Avoid unconscious, repetitive mannerisms (common ones
are slight swaying or using certain phrases on too many
occasions), if you possibly can. The honest feedback you
sought from your rehearsal audience should have alerted
your attention to these.

Keep an eye on the time. Make some quick decisions about
whether you need to speed up or slow down your delivery.

As a final quality check to your delivery, concentrate upon
the following:

S is for **Start at the start** – outline what you intend to cover.

I is for **Inject** a positive and confident style.

M is for **Monitor** the time.

P is for **Project with some passion** in your voice.

L is for go **Light on laughter** and **Leave it** to comedians,
unless you are a very confident and experienced presenter
who can gauge the mood of his or her audience well.
Humour can backfire or fall very flat.

E is for **End at the end** – summarise your main points in a
succinct conclusion.

How do I deal with difficult assessors' questions?

You can 'buy' yourself some valuable seconds of thinking
time by using one or more of the following: pausing for a few
seconds before answering (it will seem like a lifetime to you
but it will not be nearly so noticcable to the audience); taking
a short sip of water; and repeating back the main essence of
the question before you respond.

Reflect on any questions your practice audience raised with you when you did your 'dummy run', and roughly plan your responses should the same themes be raised by the assessors.

I feel very rusty on my presentation technique. Can you give me some practice topics?

Have a look again at the two topics that were mentioned as examples of 'non-technical' topics:

- My finest moment
- My greatest achievement

For each, think about STAR – what was the situation? What did I do? What happened? What was the outcome?

Convey in your presentation what was so special to you about the events that you are describing. The STAR format will assist with the structure of your delivery.

Other topics (of a semi-technical nature) to practice include:

- If appointed to this job, what would you hope to achieve during the first 3 months in the role?
- What are the main opportunities and challenges facing our organisation?
- How do you measure your success at work?
- How do you get the best out of other people at work?

Summary

Today we have looked at Presentation Exercises. We have reviewed how presentations consist of three phases – preparation, delivery, and subsequent questions. You can equip yourself to deal with the challenges of each part. We have shown that keeping your delivery SIMPLE can help you to present well at this crucial part of an Assessment Centre.

Preparing for Analysis Exercises

Introduction to Analysis Exercises

Analysis Exercises feature regularly in Assessment Centres and are not necessarily restricted to appointments for more senior roles.

Like interviews, Analysis Exercises can take many different shapes and forms. Unlike interviews and presentations, however, your scope for preparation may be quite limited. Instead, the key to your success will lie with your approach to the particular exercise on the day.

Today we will look at the different types of Analysis Exercises that you may be asked to complete in an Assessment Centre and our top tips will enable you to perform to the best of your ability.

What exactly is an Analysis Exercise?

In an Analysis Exercise, you are given a specific 'bundle' of information, and you are set a task relating to that information.

The information
This is usually in the form of documents such as memos, notes, correspondence and/or a general background briefing on a fictitious situation.

The information overall sets a particular scene, or 'simulation', rather like we discussed with Group Exercises on Tuesday, which may or may not bear a resemblance to the role for which you are applying.

Often you are asked to imagine that you are a member of the management team (sometimes stepping in at short notice to cover for an ill or absent colleague), or that you are a Consultant who advises a fictitious organisation.

The amount and complexity of the information will depend upon the level of role for which you are applying, and the Competencies which are being assessed. Increasingly these days, the information includes print-outs of e-mails, and the information itself may be presented on a computer screen.

The task
Again this will vary, but you may be asked to do one or a combination of the following:

1 To prioritise the issues represented within the information, distinguishing between what may be of relevance and importance from that which is less so
2 To analyse the information and arrive at some judgements or conclusions based upon it
3 To propose particular actions based upon your analysis
4 To present some sort of summary or report on your findings, either in a written form and/or as a presentation; look upon whatever is being submitted and assessed as your 'key output(s)'.

WARNING

Analysis Exercises come by many different names and forms, and their length can vary from approximately 45 minutes to 2–3 hours (for the most senior roles).

Look out in the timetable for phrases such as 'In-Tray Exercise' or 'In-Basket Exercise'. These both refer to the same type of exercise, in which a file of notes, memos and documents needs to be 'processed' in whatever way the instructions state. Key outputs here, for example, may be to prioritise the items and make a list of action points. Other commonly used formats are 'Analysis-Report Writing Exercise' and 'Analysis-Presentation Exercise', reflecting the different key outputs which can be sought: a report or a presentation.

Typical Competencies assessed by Analysis Exercises

You will remember from Sunday that the exercises in an Assessment Centre are selected to provide an opportunity for candidates to display the relevant Competencies. We outlined that exact Competency definitions will vary from organisation to organisation and from role to role, and that the more you can find out about the Competencies, the Job and Person Specification, the better. If you cannot get hold of that information, do not lose heart – below are some Competencies that may be assessed during Analysis Exercises.

The assessment is likely to be based upon: how you analysed or responded to the content of the Analysis Exercise, bearing in mind that there may not be a single 'right' or 'wrong' answer; how well and how clearly you delivered those responses; and how much you got done within the time constraints imposed upon you.

- **Planning and organising**
- **Persuasive communications**
- **Analysing and solving problems**

For each of these three Competencies, refer to the fuller descriptions in Appendix 1.

The above Competencies will tend to be assessed regardless of the exact content of the Analysis Exercise. Other Competencies may or may not be assessed, depending upon how 'technical' or 'high level' the material or task is. For example, senior managerial Analysis Exercises may well include a 'Strategic thinking' Competency.

Common concerns and top tips

Some of the most commonly asked questions and our top tips are shown below:

You said that the preparation I can do is limited. Is there anything, though, which I can do beforehand to help me on the day?

Firstly, think about any general skills gaps you may have. For example, some Analysis Exercises include numerical data as an element of the briefing information. If working with numbers is not your strongest point, try to brush up on things like working with percentages, ratios and fractions so that these do not trip you up on the day.

In addition, take a closer look at any statistical tables, graphs and basic accounting information that you can get your hands on, particularly where these are accompanied by supporting narrative information. The business supplements in the quality Sunday papers, magazines such as the Economist, and sets of accounts are all good sources.

Identify any knowledge gaps you may have which could be exposed by a 'technical' Analysis Exercise – namely, an exercise that may be based upon technical or professional knowledge underpinning the job that you have applied for. Perhaps this would be a good time to get a 'refresher' text down from your bookshelf.

What tips can you give me to help me do the Analysis Exercise once it begins?

Before you begin, make sure you know the answers to the following:

- What are you expected to do?
- What exactly is being assessed – for example, is it just the report you have been asked to do? Or will your supporting or 'rough' workings also be looked at?
- What Competencies/technical areas are you being assessed against in this Exercise?
- How long do you have?
- Can you split up, or mark/highlight the briefing papers to help you?

If you have any doubts – ask before the exercise begins.

Regardless of the exact nature of the key outputs sought – whether a report or a presentation, for example – you will need to manage yourself effectively through planning your work, familiarisation with the materials and then meeting those 'key outputs'.

Planning
Once the exercise begins, plan out what you need to do. Allocate time to the key elements, ensuring that you leave long enough to actually meet the key outputs, whether writing a report, submitting action points etc.

WARNING

Once you have allocated your time – stick to it! It is crucial to allow enough time to do justice to the key outputs. An all-too-common trap is to spend too long familiarising yourself with the materials. The key is to stick to the timings you set yourself.

Familiarisation
If you need to familiarise yourself with a particularly large
collection of briefing materials, make sure you at least 'skim-
sift' all the materials first. Remember, all the important or
priority issues are unlikely to be in the very first few items
you read. Therefore, do not spend too long reading the
lower-priority items and concentrate instead on the more
important areas.

As you become more familiar with the materials, identify any
links and connections in the data, perhaps making a rough
note of these as you think of them, remembering to
communicate your awareness of the relevant ones in your
key outputs.

Meeting the key outputs
If you are being asked to supply specific action points in
response to issues, be as specific as you can. Tell the assessor
who exactly you would involve, to what purpose, and why.
Avoid comments that are unspecific such as 'Have a meeting
to discuss' or 'File'.

Try to communicate to the assessor that you feel a real sense
of responsibility and controlled urgency towards resolving
the major issues in question, and that you are aware of the
implications of your proposed actions.

Clearly flag up to the assessors in your submitted work if you feel that you have had to make particular assumptions about the materials.

Avoid wasting time on overly lengthy or unfocused 'scene setting' in your final report or presentation – but make sure that you have a proper introduction and a clear conclusion.

Give appropriate rationale to support or explain your conclusions or findings. This need only be brief, focused explanatory comment, integrated into your work. However, having an identifiable 'trail' linking the material to your findings will help the assessor to appreciate your train of thought on particular points, and to assess your submissions fairly.

As a closing thought, if you can drive, can you remember your driving test when you had to make those slightly exaggerated movements of 'mirror – signal – manoeuvre'? It is the same with Analysis Exercises – not just being competent, but doing what you can to help the assessor to *see* your competence!

Summary

Today we have concentrated on Analysis Exercises. We have seen that, although Analysis Exercises can vary greatly in terms of length and content, you can make a real difference by using our top tips for successful familiarisation, planning and delivery in an Assessment Centre.

Pulling it all together

It is Saturday morning and what a week it has been! All the fears and concerns of the unknown have disappeared. Your appetite has returned with a vengeance – and the cornflakes taste great!

You look again at the letter inviting you to the Assessment Centre. With your preparation for each individual exercise under way, it is now time to pull it all together with the following thoughts:

- What general hints and tips should you follow before the Assessment Centre takes place?
- What general hints and tips should you follow during the Assessment Centre?
- What general hints and tips should you follow after the Assessment Centre?

General hints and tips before the Assessment Centre

I've just received my invite to an Assessment Centre. What should I do first?

First and foremost, check to see if a briefing or information pack is included with the letter. If not, ask if further information will be forwarded.

Read the Pack carefully, and make sure you are clear on the following points:

- What exercises can I expect?
- What Competencies are being assessed?
- Where and when is the Assessment Centre?
- What is the dress code?

Also, action any requests, for example, confirming attendance or forwarding information in advance (such as certificates). Then, make a very clear check-list of which exercises and activities you need to prepare for in advance of the Assessment Centre, as covered previously in this book.

If not covered in the information pack, make an educated guess about the Competencies that you are likely to be assessed on and the exercises you can expect on the day. Remember, if you feel that you require more information or clarification – ask.

I have special requirements – what should I do?

If you have any special requirements – including disability, dietary or other – contact the organisation. Organisations will look to make any adjustments that are reasonable, in order to ensure that no one is at a disadvantage. If you wear glasses, contact lenses, hearing aids etc. – bring them.

What should I take to the Assessment Centre?

If there is a numerical element to the day, pack your calculator (check if it needs a new battery).

Always take along a spare CV and a copy of your original application. You may meet assessors who would find it helpful to see your documents on the day.

Always take a watch – time is a critical issue at an Assessment Centre.

Have some spare paper or a small reporter's notepad to write down key names, times and learning points that you want to record for the future.

What advice can you give me about the travel arrangements?

Find out exactly where the event will be held and ensure that you get there in plenty of time. Remember to allow extra time if the venue is in a town centre, or is on a Monday morning, or if you are generally unfamiliar with the location.

If your journey is a particularly long one, ask the organisation if they are prepared to consider overnight accommodation for you.

If you are driving, make sure that you know where to park and if parking spaces are available.

What about the night before?

Try to get a good night's sleep!

General hints and tips during the Assessment Centre

What if I'm not clear about something during the day?

Do not be afraid to ask questions if you are unclear about any points – understanding the instructions is not part of the assessment!

I've heard stories that there might be 'hidden assessment' during Assessment Centres.

Be aware that you may be assessed throughout the day. This could take place over coffee, lunch or dinner, and even during a site tour.

Whenever you are in the presence of an assessor or a member of staff there is the potential for being assessed. Be on your best behaviour from the moment you walk through the door, until you leave the site at the end of the day.

How can I do my best to 'look the part' during the day?

Be alert throughout the day to your body language – your facial expressions, eye contact and mannerisms. Are they communicating what you would want them to communicate?

Dress code should be covered in the briefing pack. However, if not, phone to ask. In the event that you are unable to ascertain the dress code, always opt for normal but comfortable business attire.

Any final advice?

No matter how unfamiliar the exercises may appear, always enter into the spirit of the day. Remember, the Assessment Centre is an opportunity for you to show your capabilities. Make sure you make the most of it.

Do not try to play an unnatural role during the day that you would be unable to sustain. Instead, trust in the preparation you have done and feel confident in the skills you can offer.

Try not to panic if an exercise does not go as well as you would like. Remember it is the whole day that will be taken into account. Moreover it is a well-known fact that no one is perfect! Instead, make a note on your pad (or commit to memory) the areas where you feel you could do better next time.

Finally, switch your mobile phone off!

General hints and tips after the Assessment Centre

How can I get the most from my Assessment Centre experience?

Look back over any notes that you may have taken (written down or in your memory). Consider each exercise and think about:

- What did I do well?
- What could I do even better next time?

Also reflect on how the other candidates performed and what you could learn from their approach to the day overall, and in specific exercises.

Finally, ask for feedback from the organisation, regardless of whether you were ultimately successful or not. Compare their observations on your performance with your own notes from the day.

IN CLOSING

Assessment Centres offer a great opportunity for you to give your best, as well as to find out more about the organisation and the role. In just one week, you have done all of the preparation necessary to ensure that you are ready to succeed at an Assessment Centre.

The only final ingredient we would add is – best wishes and good luck!

Useful addresses

The British Psychological Society (BPS), 48 Princess Road East, Leicester. LE1 7DR. Tel: 0116 254 9568.

The Chartered Institute of Personnel and Development (CIPD), CIPD House, Camp Road, London. SW19 4UX. Tel: 020 8971 9000.

The Chartered Management Institute, Management House, Cottingham Road, Corby, Northants. NN17 1TT. Tel: 01536-204 222.

Further reading

Lewis, Gareth and Crozier, Gene (2002) *Psychometric Testing in a week*, 2nd edition, Hodder & Stoughton.

Peel, Malcolm and Lamb, Jon (2002) *Presentations in a week*, 3rd edition, Hodder & Stoughton.

Straw, Alison and Shapiro, Mo (2002) *Succeeding at Interviews in a week*, 3rd edition, Hodder & Stoughton.

Professional and Managerial Competency definitions

Analysing and solving problems

Positive indicators:

- Identifies the core issues of a problem
- Accurately analyses facts and figures
- Explores a range of options/solutions to the problem
- Anticipates potential obstacles
- Makes logical judgments

Commercial awareness

Positive indicators:

- Understands and applies core financial management principles (i.e. cashflow, revenue, margins, return on investment, and debtors)
- Is customer-orientated in everything they do
- Knows who the competitors are and what they are doing
- Identifies opportunities to maximise profit
- Perceives opportunities for new business

Creativity

Positive indicators:

- Comes up with new ideas and workable alternatives
- Thinks flexibly, makes unusual links between issues
- Is prepared to use less conventional methods
- Generates imaginative ideas
- Is prepared to experiment

Decision making

Positive indicatorss:

- Is prepared to make decisions in unclear or ambiguous situations
- Accepts responsibility for decisions
- Makes decisions quickly
- Takes a calculated risk
- Does not exceed decision-making authority

Leadership

Positive indicators:

- Motivates others to reach goals
- Accepts responsibility for the actions of the team
- Encourages others to take responsibility
- Provides direction, focusing team members on goals
- Leads by example

Flexibility

Positive indicators:

- Reacts positively to change
- Enthusiastically drives through change
- Adapts own behaviour to suit different individuals and situations
- Is prepared to change own views
- Is open to new methods and technologies

Integrity

Positive indicators:

- Respects company values
- Is fair in dealings with others
- Maintains ethical standards
- Does what they say they would/will do
- Respects sensitive and confidential information

Relating to others

Positive indicators:

- Respects and shows consideration to others
- Acknowledges the ideas and contributions of others
- Actively helps and supports others
- Shows tolerance towards others
- Is sociable and approachable

Planning and organising

Positive indicators:

- Prepares in advance for short and medium term
- Creates effective schedules, sets and monitors objectives and time-scales
- Prioritises work accurately
- Meets deadlines
- Plans for changing circumstances

Persuasive communications

Positive indicators:

- Communicates clearly, both orally and in writing
- Speaks confidently on both a one-to-one and group level
- Utilises facts and information to influence others
- Promotes own ideas
- Convinces others and wins them round to own point of view

Quality driven

Positive indicators:

- Knows what standards need to be achieved
- Pays attention to quality issues
- Maintains quality standards
- Sets high standards
- Achieves high quality results

Self-motivation and resilience

Positive indicators:

- Is calm and relaxed
- Remains upbeat, despite set-backs
- Is motivated by a challenge
- Is enthusiastic
- Shows drive and determination to get results

Strategic thinking

Positive indicators:

- Considers longer-term impact
- Perceives wider implications of actions
- Demonstrates a broad-based understanding of issues
- Is aware of broader market trends
- Links own and team's objectives to broader business goals.

STAR INTERVIEW TEMPLATE

For the Competency of . . .

What was the situation?

What tasks had to be done?

What actions did you take?

What was the result?

SUN

MON

TUE

WED

THU

FRI

SAT

For information

on other

IN A **WEEK** titles

go to

www.inaweek.co.uk